Marcy Schaaf

Joe Brings "Supper"

Welcome to Flint, Michigan, a place where community spirit thrives, and every day is filled with laughter and love. At the heart of this bustling town is Joe, a man known for his infectious laugh, warm heart, and unforgettable traditions.

Every spring, Joe begins an adventure that has become legendary in his family. He brings home two baby turkeys, names them Supper and Dinner, and raises them with as much love and care as any family pet. But Joe's turkeys aren't just for show—they play a special role in teaching his family about the importance of understanding where our food comes from and appreciating the cycle of life.

Through fun-filled visits to his siblings' homes, Joe, Supper, and Dinner create cherished memories that last a lifetime. Each Thanksgiving, as the family gathers, they remember the joy these turkeys brought and the lessons they taught.

"Joe Brings 'Supper'" is a heartwarming tale of family, tradition, and the bonds that connect us all. So, turn the page and join Joe on his gobbling good adventures—filled with laughter, love, and a little bit of Thanksgiving magic.

Copyright @ Marcy Schaaf 2024
Books By Schaaf
Joe Brings "Supper"

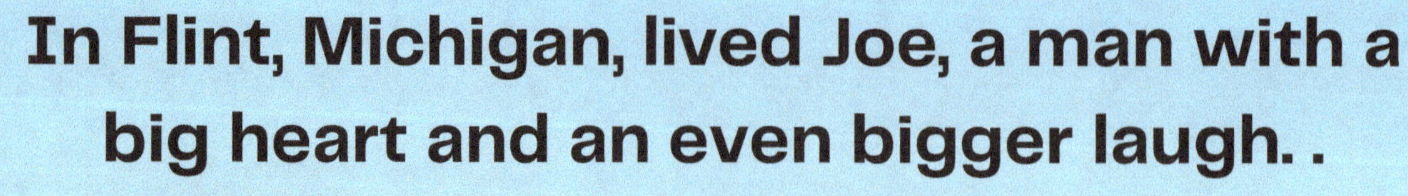

In Flint, Michigan, lived Joe, a man with a big heart and an even bigger laugh. .

Every spring, he got two baby turkeys
and named them Supper and Dinner

Joe didn't just raise turkeys; he treated them like pets!

Supper and Dinner had cozy beds, the best food, and even got bubble baths.

"Good morning, Supper!
Good morning, Dinner!"
Joe would cheer every day.

One day, Joe had a hilarious idea. He decided to take Supper and Dinner on a grand tour to his family's houses.

First stop: his sister Laura's place. "Surprise!" Joe called, holding Supper and Dinner on leashes.

Laura and her kids
laughed and pet the
turkeys.

Next, Joe visited his
brother's house.
The kids were thrilled!

Supper and Dinner loved all the attention and gobbled gleefully.

Joe's turkey visits became a
family tradition.

Everyone looked forward to
seeing Supper and Dinner
each year.

As Thanksgiving neared, Joe
knew it was time for Supper
and Dinner's final contribution.

He made sure they were
honored and treated with care.

On Thanksgiving Day,
the house was filled with delicious
smells.

"Where are Supper and Dinner?" the kids asked.

Joe smiled and said,
"They're right here making
our feast special."

Joe carved the turkey, sharing funny stories about Supper and Dinner. Everyone laughed and enjoyed the meal.

Joe told his family, "It's important to understand where our food comes from. Supper and Dinner were raised with love and care, and they are part of the food cycle."

Joe made it a point to create fun, lasting memories with his family.

A lesson he learned from his own parents

After dinner, Joe announced, "Next spring, I'll get new turkeys!" The kids cheered (well Chris did anyway) excited for more turkey adventures.

Joe's tradition continued, bringing
joy, laughter, and lessons about
love and gratitude.

It reminded everyone that meat is part
of the food cycle and should be raised in
a loving, healthy way.

Every Thanksgiving, the Schaaf family toasted to Joe, Supper, and Dinner remembering the fun and love they shared.

And so, in Flint, Michigan, Joe's turkey adventures became a cherished family legend, bringing smiles and laughter.

Happy Thanksgiving
The end!

The real Joe Schaaf visiting his nephews with "Supper"

Books By Schaaf

www.BookBySchaaf.com

Find us at:

Available at
amazon